"I have known Sporty King for most of my life, we attended junior high school together in Harlem and were neighbors. I have followed his career in marketing and in writing, both of which demonstrated great creativity and resourcefulness, but more importantly relevance. Sporty speaks not from the mouth but from the heart, the soul. He is a latter day poet in the genre of Gil Scott Heron but softer; Amiri Baraka (LeRoi Jones) but less strident; and inspirational as James Weldon Johnson. He is a poet for our times, troubles, fears and fantasies. He speaks in a beat that is today. He's Harlem's gift to the world—the next 'Beat Poet.'"

—Nat Queen, London

"An uplifting gumbo of positive thoughts and vibrations that bring into focus, living in the moment, and embracing the wonderful journeys of life. Readers will rejoice in their own moments, and transcend their own thinking about the notion of merely existing. A wonderful collection that is beautiful in it's simplicity."

—Pam "Mocha Sistah" Osbey, Osbey Books

Author of *Black Orchids* and *Musings of a Mocha Sista*

Dan + Beth
Cheers + Toasts + Tall Tails
to you for being real...

Your Name Came to Mind

By Sporty King

Sporty 11/3/12

PublishAmerica
Baltimore

© 2006 by Sporty King.
All rights reserved. No part of this book may be reproduced, stored in a retrieval system or transmitted in any form or by any means without the prior written permission of the publishers, except by a reviewer who may quote brief passages in a review to be printed in a newspaper, magazine or journal.

First printing

At the specific preference of the author, PublishAmerica allowed this work to remain exactly as the author intended, verbatim, without editorial input.

ISBN: 1-4241-0920-5
PUBLISHED BY PUBLISHAMERICA, LLLP
www.publishamerica.com
Baltimore

Printed in the United States of America

In 1995 I wrote *I Found Out I'm Dying: A Celebration of Life in Spoetry*. It's amazing how many people missed the subtitle... ultimately missing the message. After writing that book I began a wonderful journey and test of my faith. The challenge of marketing a speaking career based on the use of poetry took me on a roller coaster ride of fear and joy. It was during that ride that I grew and came to the realization of my deep belief in God and myself. That ride took me through Chapter 13 & 7 bankruptcies, foreclosure on my house, automobile repossession, *used-car flashbacks*, real estate and income tax troubles...

I mention this up front because I won't spend time discussing it throughout the book. You see, these twists, turns and *drops* on the ride reminded me just how wonderful this gift of life is. They reminded me of just how alive I am. And that we must all recognize and remember that what we most enjoy about the roller coaster is the *drop*.

For we are all masters of change.

And what you'll find throughout this book is ammunition to connect you with your individual *mastery*, as my *story* is inspired by people from different walks of life who help me stay the path...

I Found out I'm Dying

Actually, I've known it for quite some time now
But for so many others its new news.
So I'd like to thank You (God) for yesterday
As much as I do for today.

And I ask that you (my friend) pause, but not stop,
To think about some of the wild things I've survived
Before my greatest challenge…and believe me,
Death is the only challenge we won't sit and laugh about
[Or relive]

But we can find joy in it,
Because there'll be enough kind words to create a new dictionary.
Kind words that I need now, more than ever

Kind words keep us alive
Physically…mentally…spiritually.

I found out I'm dying
And when I woke this morning I wept.
And I laughed aloud and I started to sing
(but remembered that I couldn't, so I danced instead)
And I whistled a tune as I made my bed

I threw open the window and let out a cheer
(actually I just smiled, so no one could hear)

I exercised, ate and dressed (after I washed)
Then I looked in the mirror and gave a wink.
*"Not bad for a body that's survived another day,
I'm so blessed to get older"*
Is all I could think.

I didn't bother reading the Obituary
(Because I knew I wasn't there)
Instead I clipped my fingernails…and neatly styled my hair

I found out I'm dying
And that I have been since Day Number One.
So I spend little time regretting my life
Because I'd rather spend the time having fun.

I Found out I'm Living

Actually, I've known it for quite some time now
Yet only at a surface level.
And, again, I thank you (God) for yesterday,
as much as I do for today.

And I ask that you (my friends) join me
in recognizing that the challenge
of this roller coaster ride called "life"
is even greater when you take responsibility
for your actions and self.

For as I am able to look at where I was, and what I did
It becomes more evident to me who I am.
And through that realization I extend my hand to touch you
Actually to feel you
Because in my position as *Conduit of Good Spirits*
The physicality of our sharing pales in comparison
To how and why we must love one another.

I found out I'm living.
And when I woke up this morning I praised that vision
That I might be allowed to ride His coat tails
And see Him in my every decision.

I sat by the window and took in another breath
For somewhere…somehow…someone…didn't.
So I checked my five, for their alignment with my sixth sense
Thus my ability to
experience…experience…experience…experience…experience…

While my smile sent a flush of joy to every tip
Of this temporary body I occupy
And came back in an unspoken word of comfort.

I read the Word to exorcise my soul of fear.
I recognized what others called miracles
As the blessings that were always there
I found out I'm living
And that I have been since Day Number One.
Yet it was not until I released my physical self
That I was really able to give God the glory
And thanks for all that I've done

Contents

I Found out I'm Dying 7
I Found out I'm Living 9
Today I Took a Moment 15
Invisible Light 17
I Thought I Was Ready 19
I Don't Feel It…Because I'm Excited 20
Giving Thanks 21
Predicting the Past 22
From My Limited Scope 24
It's Easy to Run Away 25
My Rainbow Is Real 27
Needless to Say 30
Class Acts 32
Life, Love & Laughter… 34
The Wings of W.O.R.D.S. 36
The Spirit of W.O.R.D.S. 37
Saved by the Bell 38
A Day in the Life Of… 39
I Step for Success… 41
Budding in Excellence 42
The Courageous Eight 43
Basket Case 44
Can You Only See Me When I'm Down? 46
We've All Got Power 47
Necessary, by Every Means Possible 48
If I Could Fly 50
Breaking the Chain 51
The Journey Within 53
Creating a New You 54
Feeling at Peace with Me 55
New Life 56

Two for Shore	57
Pressure: A Thing of the Past	58
I Can't Save the World…But I Can Save You.	59
Love's Merry-Go-Round	62
God's Love	64
Forgetting the Future…	65
Seasoned with JOY	67
Seniors Only	68
Love Equals Peace	69
Holy Rosa	71
Renaissance Woman	72
Turning Points	73
Women	75
Flame of Life	76
Thirst for Life	77
Respect	78
Reign of Excellence	79
Giving	80
Young Prophets	83
Giving a Stand	85
Proclaim the Victory	88
Beauty Is in the "I"	90
Every Life, a Young Life	91
I Am Here Today	92
I'm Thinking about You Today.	94
Friendship Questioned & Answered	95
Friendship Disguised as Love	96
State of Mind	97
What Happens When We Leave God Out of Love?	99
Power Unveiled	101
How Far Is the Middle?	102
The Wish	104
Cloudy Daze	105

Levels of Presidency	107
Silent Fanfare	109
I Miss Me	110
Thanks-Living	112

Today I Took a Moment

Today I took a moment to enjoy my life.

Didn't map it out too tough
Made no guidelines to success.

Put no time limit on it
No expectations…

…I just enjoyed it (I must confess)

Soaked in some sun,
heard smiles, felt my name.
My moment was a journey, an exchange
For as my spirit lifted
to enjoy this higher plane,
I found myself, a child again.
I just enjoyed it (I must exclaim)

Didn't stop to worry about paying a bill.
No responsibility…no aches & pains…
really no time to kill.

Today I took a moment to enjoy my life
I looked around,
counted each blessing I could find.
Then I looked for blessings I couldn't see.

Your name came to mind.

Spiritual growth is the base and most fulfilling aspect of recognizing the blessing in your gift of life. Crucial in recognizing that gift is understanding the power we each possess to take steps toward making our lives fun. That power manifests itself most when we can minimize the negative impulses surrounding us in the forms of people or situations. In fact, my 1997 started out with my family's losing our second child in as many years. At the funeral, I dedicated *INVISIBLE LIGHT* to by brother, Landy, while reminding the congregation that we all need invisible light...

Hence, while so many people felt they "...*had to be at the funeral*...," I reminded them that only Landy *had* to be there. Unfortunately, so many of us only get in touch with our mortality after the loss of another. My tribute went on to be heartfelt, entertaining, and representative of our family's spirit of celebration.

Invisible Light

The Lord is my Shepherd
I should not want…but I do!

I want to see His light
To reach up and touch praise
To lean forward and taste salvation
To perk up and hear glory
To lean back and smell peace
To open up and see resurrection.

See, my walk has never been a straight line.

My path has twisted, turned, tripped and stopped
And my burning has always won new layers of faith

    strengthening my Armor
    blessing my Blood
    christening my Consciousness

And as the ABC's of my life turn to G.O.D.'s
The smile in my spirit is renewed
And my want for light
Becomes need.

A large part of that need is in recognizing the blessing in just waking up each day. A blessing that is among those we take for granted, often allowing ourselves to overlook it in favor of material prosperity…a prosperity that means nothing without faithful introspection.

I Thought I Was Ready

The guest list boasted so many names
I wondered if mine didn't need to be on it.

I had chosen the right silverware and china...
(Mikasa...Pukasa...Whokasa?)
The fabric was lush and decoratively colored...
(Glorious Gold...Prosperous Purple...Bountiful Blue)

Music was in place...
(Jazz...Soft & Smooth)
Finest menu spiced with sweet and sour delicacies
That were complimented by an assortment of wines
And refreshing beverages.
I was so excited that I went to bed without saying my prayers.

Instead I went to sleep thinking about the gifts and trips...
(Pairs...Sets...Assortments...)
How well I had planned everything...

And I can now understand
That God gave me a different blessing that day...

See, I thought I was ready
Yet, He had not planned to wake me up.

I Don't Feel It...
Because I'm Excited

Can you imagine being there?
Especially the first time you understood the significance?
It was like a dream come true
(light bulbs flashing . fireworks . just noise . noise . noise)

All of your favorite people, foods and colors
were all around you celebrating
the trials & tribulations eclipsed with unconscious ease.
(no) Joy!

Joy that shielded you from the cold, the rain,
the lies & threats...
(Dare you consider the joy of pain?)

Can you just imagine the electric sensation of sunrays
Heating up your brow . parching your mouth
. that tingle in your stomach .
the newness of the voices welcoming and urging you on?

Each step a monument or testament of tenacity.
Every movement an unconscious dance with necessity.
The fragrance . the breeze . the spinning excitement in the room
. the challenge of doing it again.
Just imagine!

Of course, there are also times where I wake up
and don't feel blessed to do so.

Giving Thanks

You won't recognize the angel
His language will be too frank
When you really get God's help
You won't know who you should thank.

So make your decision to give thanks now
Keep Him worthy of your praise
Don't try to figure out His motives
For ours are not His ways.

Have you wondered how you sounded
asking for, while wasting life?
Or have you simply taken for granted
that you can do as you please
and not suffer consequence...
until you get tired and decide to
seek His help by reflex...
call out His name by habit...
question your penance?

Have you lost your place on the Implementation Crew,
forgetting that only He is on the Planning Committee,
and blinded yourself with jealously and selfishness?

Oh, my brethren, I beg that you do not surround yourself
with the worldly misgivings and short comings
that hoist you atop a throne that can no longer touch the hearts
that call for your guidance.

See, you won't recognize the Angel
Nor His concern for your health.
When you really want God's help
Let that Angel be yourself

Predicting the Past

I have looked back at my life often...
And, if you'd like, I can look back at yours
And I noticed I overcame great obstacles...
Yet it surprised me who opened the doors...

For the most impactful lessons I learned...
Came from those I had given my back
From persons I thought I had no need for...
Who eventually helped me question my tact:
The ex-girlfriends, other ethnicities and lifestyles
(I'll keep this list short so I can finish this poem)

The hatred, anger and ignorance, nonchalance, arrogance and lies,
cheating, stealing and pain
(I had to list these shortcomings, for through the lessons they taught,
I now recognize my old life as insane).

You see, back then there were a lot of first-time reactions involved
And my immaturity allowed me to fall short.
I could shift the blame and hide behind excuses...
(Now there's a list far too long to report)

Back then each person I met started out as a stranger
Whose intentions I questioned (instead of my own)
It was so much easier to see their faults, while leaving mine alone

Their selfishness was clear, they were out to please only themselves
Yet, all I had to share, was neatly stacked on my hidden shelves.

I valued only my opinion with no regard for their seeing the light
Flexibility bounced out the window, I could only see me being right.

I followed the crowd, and sometimes I led it...
ridiculed and poked fun at this one and that.
As they say now (back then) I was a Bag of Chips...
Oh, yes, I was really all THAT

Oh, don't get me wrong, it's still all about me
The difference is in how I now define myself,
and the truth that has set me free

Because I now understand my need to be a man
I can thank those ex-girlfriends for the patience they somehow lived:
Dealing with my insecurities and my inability,
(No, my unwillingness) to find a way to give.

The prejudice I entertained kept me frozen in negativity
I took the time to harden my heart
I found ways to be "down" and "get over"
All the while thinking that I was so smart.

And my brothers and sisters who didn't mirror me on either side
(inse or outse)
are now welcome parts of my life for just that reason.
Yes, now I recognize how lonely and lost I would be
if everywhere I turned I saw only me...

And, who knows, maybe I just needed some of "those" people
...to make me exercise those negative emotions
...to help me see how I felt about myself...

In fact, I predict: that that's exactly what happened...

From My Limited Scope

Shall I call the Psychic NOT-Line?
Or have my palm blue?
Or would it be better if I do all I can
To find out about myself, based on what I hear from you?

You're the man who understands menstrual cramps...
The winner who says you've never lost...
The woman who forgot to wear an athletic support cup...
The fresh-out-of-college boss...

The black who's never been white,
The left that's never been right.
You've always lived in the same place
Never traveled or visited afar
Never flown or taken the train
And you never have driven a car.

Didn't marry, no kids, not a drink or drug have you taken.
The son who's never been a daughter,
Yet you freely give your opinion with authority
And act as if it's you who walked on water.

Now, from where I sit I cannot answer every question,
In fact, there are times where I'll add to what is asked.
For as similar as my experiences are, they're different
So understanding, rather than answering, becomes my task.

It's Easy to Run Away

But when the run is over,
all of our problems catch up.
And as we put the brakes on,
we relive the discomfort from each jolt
as we flashback to our *escape*.

All of the *free* time
we visualized, fantasized, internalized
turns to lies
as we question the hue of green
surrounding the grass upon which we now feast.

A feast whose nourishment we pray
will lift the veil from our past
to, instead, confirm and justify our act(s) of desperation
(or are they just reactions to despair?)

Yes, we cling to our claim that we gave our all
That we did our best
Though, secretly, we protest any notion
that we cannot reach a higher level.

We banish the *What Ifs…Who Knows…*and *Why Dids*
To embellish *So What…Anyhow…*and *Told You So*

Summoning our highest human-ness
we block the thoughts that serve
as nothing but reminders of suffrage and pain
Though they could serve
as realization points in our growth and understanding
of who we are.

See, it's easy to run away.
It's hard to know when to leave.

Speaking of leaving…if you noticed in my *Foreword*, I used the term "automobile repossession" rather than "having my car repossessed." Among the definitions of the prefix *re* is the notion of *gaining again*. Thus you can only repossess something that originally (or actually) belonged to you. When I surrendered the car I was driving, I realized it was not *my* car. And I sat down on *my* couch and looked at *my* TV, listened to *my* stereo before going to sleep in *my* bed and dealing with *my* challenge the next day. A challenge, like most, that was but one among many I can look back upon and smile. You can probably think of some hurdles you've overcome. What's more important is that you take conscious time to forgive yourself. That's the message I shared, and continue to share, with audiences of all ages.

One such audience was a group of teenagers at an alternative high school. Alternative high schools serve students that are pushed out or drop out of traditional schools. Many of these students just don't fit into the straight and narrow of high school. They may have no family support; may be financially assisting their families; are wards of the State or from orphanages; are spoiled little rich kids; many are 19-21 years old and could easily pass the G.E.D., but are simply rebellious teens that decide they do want a high school education.

During a session with a group of 23 young men and women, I offered to dedicate a poem to them. The only buy-in required was that they write their nickname and favorite color on a piece of paper. Eleven of the young ladies did so. We chose to create a poem that expressed how they felt about their lives. Because our lives must be filled with color, I painted the picture of positivity swelling in the hearts of these future leaders.

My Rainbow Is Real

It sings in bold, majestic colors
Grateful Green...Radiant Red...Prosperous Purple it's true
Glorious Gold...Berry Black...and, of course, Bountiful Blue.

See, my rainbow is real
It's vision dances on high
My success and faith are a testimony
For not every rainbow is found in the sky.

How would we live if we could start from the end?
Would we open our hearts
to appreciate the richness in life's lessons
that mean more than material wealth?
Would we open our books to only the chapters we needed
or realize that our completeness is nothing in and of itself?

Tolerance...Patience...Understanding

Oh, if we could only see how important each person
and situation will be to our success
We could laugh and enjoy the knuckleheads, jerks, liars and cheats
Knowing that they, too, are living out their destiny.
Knowing that we, too, are important to their rainbow...

Fortunately, my God does not require that I start at the end
For He has blessed me with each morning's vision
that I might flourish among His creation.

See, my rainbow is real
It sings in bold, majestic colors
Grateful Green...Radiant Red...Prosperous Purple it's true
Glorious Gold...Berry Black...and, of course, Bountiful Blue.

It's vision dances on high
My success and faith are a testimony
For not every rainbow is found in the sky.

This next poem was also written through the eyes of alternative high school students. Following that is from a group of 8th graders, and a class of 3rd graders, before my final thoughts on our youth. Each group was asked to call out words that came to their minds as we discussed the topic of the day. What's important for you to feel in these is the parallel in the thought process with what's in your heart. What did you think about when you were in your teens...or seven...?

Needless to Say

I need people in my life.
That's why I put myself in positions, places and situations
that allow me to meet that need.

Yeah, I know about being unique
I'm in touch with my gift
Somebody loves me (in fact, I do)
Yet when I look in the mirror,
the background I see is not the opulence I saw
in that dream a few nights ago.

My surroundings say
Made in [*everywhere but my name*]
And [not so] suddenly I realize that
even my God chose not to be alone.
I need people in my life.
That's why I put myself in positions, places and situations
that allow me to meet that need.

Oh, I know everybody's not gonna like me
But I ask for respect.
Somebody's gonna push me down, pull me down
Lock me up, so I can't be around
All I ask for is respect.

Because my life is precious
It ain't no joke
I'm nobody's fool, and I'm not a clown
I need people in my life.
That's why I put myself in positions, places and situations
that allow me to meet that need.

Because I see how many people need me.
Some need me to see myself as less than a man
Some want me to be a woman on my back
So they tell lies on me, cheat me, help me focus on my past
No matter how I try to get ahead
They tell me I won't last

And all I ask for is respect…
They try to rush me through the system…
Then when I'm almost through, they pull me back…
I start questioning, doubting, not believing in myself…
And I want to scream "Give me some slack" — *But I stay cool.*

I look inside myself and know that I'm here
because I'm a survivor
And there's someone behind me who needs to know what I've lived and learned.
I need all kinds of people in my life.
That's why I put myself in key positions,
high places and the best situations I can think of to meet that need.
Because I respect myself.

Class Acts

...What each of you truly are...What most of us strive to be...
I thank you for bringing new challenge into my life
Your affect was far more than you could see.
For, each smile, every round of applause (even the teeth sucking)
Reminded me of my youth...A memory that confirms my growth.

Sure, it may seem like 100 years ago
And what you call *'Bout It*...We called *Cool*.
But the message that never changes
is the reminder of hope and success:
To learn life's best lessons...You have to stay in school.

But don't just stay to take up space...Because the joke will be on you.
And it's a joke that has no punch line,
Just confusion about what to do.

You see, right now you don't need all the answers
You need questions, faith and love.
You need to believe in yourself more and more each day
And your true gang leader—the Lord up above.

For, from musty little 4 year old kids to mellow 70 year old adults
He has truly welcomed us into this family and world.
His guidance will make strong men out of little boys,
And even stronger women out of little girls.

We don't have to behave like clowns...
but we choose to sometimes,
It's safer than admitting how we feel.
At times it gives us the chance to exercise our imagination
And other times, it's just a way of *keepin' it real*.

Class Acts
…What each of you truly are…
And the secret to maturing and living to be old…
Stay focused on being your best
and making your choices right for you,
And thanks for letting me be a part of your life
During my day at the proud Black and Gold.

Life, Love & Laughter...

Life is so sweet...
Love is beautiful...
Laughter is fun.

Yet, it is the opportunity to help people
...that makes my life so special
...that makes my love so rewarding
...that makes my laughter so important
...because my joy helps people get closer to God.

I'm talking about the important people:
My family, teachers and friends,
the grandparents and cousins
in Minnesota, Tennessee, New Orleans, Mississippi, Chicago
and all the people in all the places.
I enjoy seeing smiles on all peoples' faces.

Because life is real good
In fact, it's as good as honey.
So whenever I'm feeling down, I just tickle myself
So I can laugh and love,
Because life can really be funny.

...and what do you think about now? One day, members from each of the preceding groups of youngsters will silently thank the educators who played such a key role in their lives...but they won't know where to find them.

Likewise, I don't know where to find Mr. Rush, Ms. Monroe, Mrs. Land, or Fr. Farrell. Yet, in sharing my gift with those who continue in the education field, I thank my past teachers through my appreciation for those who now carry the passion to cultivate young minds. I encourage you to thank a teacher today, for the teacher you gave "fits" and now can appreciate. These next 8 poems are written through the eyes of and finally about today's educators (both teachers and parents).

The Wings of W.O.R.D.S.

Soaring among, rather than above, the hearts We touch
Our message casts a Spirit of Wisdom and Opportunity…
Resonating with Dignity, Self-worth,
Sincerity, Determination, Reverence, Originality and Wonder.

Oh, how our flight Relaxes and Delights…
Romances and Delivers…Rejuvenates and Dives…
Synchronously Decorating and Reshaping thoughts
that enhance, encourage and allow creativity's holiness
to Shine forth and guide the majesty of today's Waking.

Our Reward: Deliciously Delicate Smiles…

We Openly Scramble to Share Wit and Wisdom,
even Weird and Silly moments that Remind us to believe.
And as we flash back to our ascension,
we Relive the patience and understanding of Mrs. Land, Mr. Rush,
parents, friends, coaches, peers and Ourselves.

Our Walk is Drenched with
Sincerity, Devotion, Realism, Organization and Wealth…
for as we take pride in elevating
Wanda, Orlando, Robert, Danielle and Sally,
we Welcome and enjoy our power, knowing that
What Others Remember and Digest Slowly
Strengthens Students.

The Spirit of W.O.R.D.S.

if you've ever had One of those Days,
consider yourself Wonderfully blessed...
as Others may have had Reason to be Dazed.
So, Smile and Show those Sensational Dimples of Responsibility,
as you Overcome the Worry, and Share your light by way of praise.

For your Will to be Obedient, Reaches Deep inside each Soul
With a nectar of Outrageous Delight and Success.
You become the Wizard Who Openly Rewards clicked heels...
you help Winners Repeat and Realize
that they are Worthy of being the best.

You Remind us that Our golden Road of Opportunity
is laced with Reality...
you're Delightfully Witty and Wise.
You enjoy Witnessing the Dynamic metamorphosis
of God's Delicate little girls and little guys.

For as their choices Stand in the face of Dangerous Options,
their Decisions crave Ordered Steps in Worship...
and your Relentless guidance Signals the Savior's touch.
It may be years before you Recognize the fruit of your labor,
yet using only your lifetime Would be far too much.

Strengthen your Desire to Retain an Omnipotent Will...
know that your Word effects every child Who hears it...
find comfort in your power and blessing
to Shape One of *these* Days,
for What Others Remember & Digest
Soothes and Strengthens Students' Spirits

Saved by the Bell

Have you ever really been…?
Or have you wondered if they thought they were…?
Sometimes the day Can go so fast
Whether you did…or didn't…becomes a blur.

Yet, rest Assured that you did Encourage a Child today
Right now some Parent is Praising your name.
Your Compassion and Empathy Empowers your Class
To navigate a Path of Ambition and fame.

Silent Appreciation, must Pump through your veins
Patience, repress the urge to scream.
An Eager Child's growth becomes reality
Because some Educator Accepted their dream.

Powerful four-letter words become 5…then 6…then 7…
The gift of Caring Creates an inner blush.
Stay Conscious and Proud of your Effect on Every life
For there are times where you're Even their first Crush.

You see, Actually you are for whom the bell tolls
(of course, if you're the music teacher [maybe] cover your ears)
And the thanks you get today is but a fraction
Of the subliminal success you reach Each year.

For, Extraordinary Engineers…Countless Cops…Average Athletes…
Emerging Entrepreneurs…and Public Politicians
Are busy being their best because you were yours.

Always know that the saving grace of the bell
Is that it rings in PEACE to open new doors.

A Day in the Life Of...

every day in the life of a Cherished Child is essential
for in those eyes is Radiant Sunshine, Hope, Independence and love
and sometimes, like a poem, there's no Rhyme or Reason
so we must Calmly give thanks for the blessing from above.

We Create a Realistic bond
that Can only grow through an Idealistic spirit
Holistically, we nurture a Healthy sense of selfhood
("*Culminatingly*" so)
enroute we find that our Inspiration to move forward
Comes from our Charismatic passion of what we know.

And because knowledge is the key
we Recognize that our Reach is for the Inner Child
where the Challenge to achieve Carries that exceptional value mix
of Resourceful, Imaginative, Childish and Hard-Headed (smile).

Because the key is knowledge
we make the Right moves toward Helping these seeds of our present grow
Reminding them that to win in their future,
the thing that's Really Cool
Is to trust our Inspiration to believe and excel in school

what we understand most is the need to Resist the temptation
to Connect outside of the Heart
so we accept our Calling with Honor
and push Harder to keep Innocent Children smart

a Romantic Calling? (not always)
yet a nonstop Chance to witness the Impact
the Invisible Reward of the Righteous:
Caring enough to give back

every day in the life of a Cherished Child is essential
and whenever I Choose to think this life is Hard
I'll look in the mirror and give myself a wink
and Remind that Image to Choose to sing Hallelujah
and give praise to Almighty God.

I Step for Success...

Suppose I were Clueless...Insensitive to Their needs?
My Children would suffer a Tremendous loss of Trust
So it's Important that I keep myself Together
My Commitment to the Vision is a must.

I must see the Victory Through my wisdom and patience
Use my Charisma, Courage and Creativity to help them grow
Be Conscious of the fact that few people get paid for what they Think
The Value is Turning that Thinking Into what you know

My pledge does not force Control of Their lives upon school Teachers
Instead we Team to develop Talent and Intelligence in every girl and boy
Together we become the Village that takes Time
To Inspire Through our labor of love and unselfish joy

Our Thirst for success is quenched in knowing the Impact we have
in bringing a smile of joy to Their lives
For we recognize ourselves as Voluptuous Idols of natural love

We understand society's quest to Entice our Children
to sink below Their True Value
It's a hurdle we've Eclipsed with God's help from above.

As God has given us Charge of that most precious life: our own
We share it to help our Children grow
We stretch our Creativity to make Connections more meaningful
And stay Conscious of being the star in our Video.

As we Continue to Teach the blessing of life by living it
The Vibrancy in our spirit Clearly states that we are the best.
We are blessed, fortunate, Introspective
and Through practice getting better
Because our each and every step is for success.

Budding in Excellence

The intensity of Social Studies
laced with the perfecting nature of Science
We're proud to say we've planted more than one see.
Yet the glory wonderfully basks in retrospect
As our young prodigies get what they want and what they need.

They grow to be robust, yet gracious models of success
And somehow they find a way to always reach back.
However silently, we rejoice, as one of their role models
Even though we don't play ball like Kobe or Shaq.

Therefore it's important for us to stay confident
To recognize and believe in ourselves
For we pass on more than a lesson plan
We create and protect "Knowledge Shelves"

Understanding is our base, as we move toward excellence
Still we never forget the blessings or the grace.
For these are weapons that arm us, to arm RGCA
Our reward is in the radiance of each face.

The Courageous Eight

Encouraged to wake up to start a fresh day
We brace ourselves to forgive
For there are plenty of times where we not only teach,
We help our students learn to live.

It's a wonderful feeling to see an occasional smile...
Pleasing to inhale the energy.
We rally to support the bright ones,
And stay positive for all each child can be.

Excellence, wisdom and outrageous success
Become immeasurable goals that test our worth
So it becomes increasingly important
That we remain passionate for every day on this side of the earth.

Our courage cannot be eaten up, but replenished
For we're no ordinary group of blessed souls.
We're the Courageous Eight Educators of Young Leaders
Our story is always seen, if never told.

Basket Case

As I recall, it was an excellent day for a tornado
And just when you start to laugh
Think about how tough it can be to be successful
With all the obstacles and challenges thrown in your path.

Yet, let me take the time to express my thanks
You see, I know you may not hear it everyday
Yet realize that as you share your talent, you do a terrific job
Of preparing students to stay focused, and not to stray.

Sure, sometimes it's a stressful situation
But (guess what?) you always manage to make it through.
So understand that basket (in this case)
Is the cushion you provide
For there'd be no Great Beginnings without you.

We cannot be in a great mood 24 hours a day, 7 days a week. My wish for you—don't have a bad day. Don't waste your possible last day, down in the doldrums. Say this aloud:

> *I can have a bad hour, or even two*
> *But my bad hour should not affect you.*
> *And having a bad day*
> *Is something I won't do.*

Catchy affirmations remind us to take the high road, and look at things from a positive viewpoint. We make choices every day. Choose to be positive.

Can You Only See Me When I'm Down?

I accomplish…I achieve…
I push hard because I believe.
You talk about the substandard education
Of someone who reminds you of me.

I manage…I own…I excel…
I'm doing better than surviving, I'm doing well.
You show someone half clothed and angry on TV
Someone who reminds you of me.

I write…I speak…I read…
I create more than I ever need.
You enjoy someone sending an ebonic "shout out" on the radio
Someone who reminds you of me.

Can I only get my point across by living in the past
Must my credibility soak in delegated feelings of guilt
Asking you to have empathy, (no) sympathy
For what I went through
with my mother, father, brothers & sisters,
jobs, homes, law, stores, buses, taxis,
in the swimming pool where I almost drowned…
Can you only see me when I'm down?
I asked of myself in the mirror.

Do I only see me when I'm down?

We've All Got Power

You've got to like Power
Power needs a home with a welcome mat
Power needs to know just where it's at
Power needs to hear its name again and again
Because Power gets stronger
(And sometimes forgets where its been)

Power doesn't have a favorite body, race or sex
Power is what you make it and
how you do what you do next.

Power doesn't broadcast reason
And, like this poem,
it's happy to give a little rhyme
But you've got to like Power
to get the most out of it and use it best…

On earth you get a taste of your Power
And when you like it, it's no longer a test.

Necessary, by Every Means Possible

A slave mentality is hereditary.

Oh, yes...
If my mother reminds me
that I'm gonna be just like my no good father
because "a black man wants a white woman when he gets some money,"
she reminds herself that she's not good enough to be a queen
or equal to a white woman,
and feeds her angry spirit that repels my attraction
and makes her less of a prize...
while reminding my sister
to lower her expectations of her son's father
(unless she's light *skin-did*).

Oh, yes...
If my father reminds me to avoid the trap he fell into
because "a black woman ain't never gonna be satisfied,"
he reminds himself that he's not fit to support a family
or be the king of his castle,
and feeds my need to define my manhood based on
the number of women I can service...
reminding my sister to be sure she gets paid
because brown sugar is as sweet as it gets,
so don't let a male call himself a man
if he can't afford to be her daughter's father
(especially one of them high *yella* boys).

And as he (the father) lives *down* to her (the mother's) expectations,
while she (the mother) keeps *up* to his (the father's) negative image,
their son and daughter misinterpret the definition
of what a man or woman is...
and unconsciously continue the cycle
while vowing not to be like their parents.

When we let go of the past, we can live in the present
and create images that allow our children to recognize the difference
between personal choice and foregone conclusion.
Let "X" mark the spot from which you'll live *your* life.

A slave mentality is hereditary.

It's necessary that you pass that *fact* on…
By every means possible.

If I Could Fly

As my euphoria sought ample footing
The myth of reality welcomed my flight
Boredom felt my wrath
Complacency experienced my scorn
Arrogance was grounded from my sight.

For my joy focused upward,
Your touch called me by name.
My spirit's voice responded
To that vision that remains the same:

That I might be allowed to flourish
Beyond their wildest dreams
To walk among the mortals
Or, at least, that's how it would seem.

My ascension would beckon the melody of trumpets
The genuflect of each diamond's edge
precipitous clouds would warm me
as the moon tanned my silhouette
And I'd climb, and I'd climb, and I'd climb effortlessly
Just to see how far I could get.

When I asked for Your hand
I banished my fear and exposed myself,
Never asking why.
Knowing that I'll reach my next plateau
And that I win because I always try.

Breaking the Chain

Chaos . Hatred . Anger . Ignorance . Negativity

When we allow ourselves to Cradle excuses
that beckon our demise,
we give power to the pain that sucks the life out of our aspirations.

While we Hold onto yesterday's darkness, we fester in our grudge,
recalling only the lies
that drag us away from the realization of our growth.

As we Accept mediocrity, we deny our worthiness of the best.
And in that denial
the plateau becomes a ledge becomes the ground
becomes below our true value.

So often we Invite adversity into our lives
by wasting the opportunity to gain knowledge.
More importantly, knowledge put to no use detracts from our faith.

Should we Nurture stereotypes,
we surrender our right to eclipse stupidity
and forfeit our claim to inherit freedom.

When we choose a chain that has no love
Our bond is with death.

Cradle your freedom
Hold onto your faith
Accept your true value
Invite your growth
Nurture your aspirations

Break the CHAIN

Willing to break that chain, were the hundreds of public aid recipients I met through various welfare-to-work programs. These programs had a mandate to re-introduce people who had been on welfare to the world of work. These next 10 poems were written through the eyes of women and men who were caught-up in the system. Human beings shackled with the stereotype of being *lazy, negative people milking the system for years...not wanting to work...wanting an easy job where they got paid for doing little or nothing...or preferring to sit and watch TV.* People, who I found, proved to be spiritual and concerned parents...some whom had only been on aid for less than a year...many nervous or, even scared of the life change on their horizon.

Yes, a life change, not a job...and as you will see, people happy to join in focusing on the positive. Each poem was created through the words of audience members. Sessions conducted all began with a theme, or word for the day. Each word was treated as an acronym, and members were asked to suggest complete positive words to satisfy each letter of the acronym. The words in either poem with capitalized first letters are those of the audience. Themes used were SELF, THANKS, LIFE, WOMEN, SOUP, BREAD and GIVING.

The Journey Within

My next Step Surprised (even) me…
on the outside it was bold without a care
my Smile…my walk…my actions
aimed at the Success so many have come to fear.

For the challenge to maintain and repeat this pace
has damaged many a Fickle Spirit and Erased a Lazy disposition.
Fortunately, my path continues to Feed
and Fulfill my Stride to Excellence through Education

And as the vision of my Fruitful ascension takes it's Shape
I Feel Empowered to describe myself
in words that Emulate my Splendor:
…Smart…Energetic…Likable…Funny…
even Stupendous…Effervescent…Luxurious and Fabulous,
as this heightened interior awareness
decorates a Lavish Exterior of Sensitivity.

My Surroundings' adjustment to my rejuvenated Lifestyle
allows itself to Freeze in its tracks
while my Focus on the prize cushions my every Step

Family, Friends and Fantasy Strengthen my commitment to Survive…
as my Search to Flourish, rather than Exist,
becomes the passion that keeps me alive.

My road widens in anticipation of the Emotional celebration
of a heart Flushed with Love. Excitement
and Stimulating thoughts of myself that Suddenly become captured
as the reality that guides my Faith-Filled Landing
in Everlasting Silence.

And, yes, this is only the beginning.

Creating a New You

While thinking about what your child
could be...should be...or would be...
Don't pass up the opportunity to ask
"And what about me?"

For yours is the gift of creation.
What you make is not easily replaced.
So take your time and enjoy yourself
Understand that all you've done won't go to waste.

For among your creations is an upgraded *You*,
someone nobody else can duplicate or be
And a part of that creation is that you recognize your voice
And your vision is of someone *You* can see.

So far you've made the moves that got you to this place called "right"
Stop to give yourself credit—it didn't happen over night.

You've been persistent, sacrificial,
even foolish (some might say).
You've proven to yourself that you're a survivor
Not concerned about winning or losing,
as much as the blessing to be able to play.

So as you prepare your basketball stars,
your firemen, nurses, doctors and lawyers,
And ask them to pass each test,
Let your "B" be sure to remind them
How important it is to be respected and always your best.

Meanwhile, know that this is not a prepared follow up...
But a follow up prepared for you.
You're important and deserve that *Queenly* treatment
Enjoy your new power and what *You* can do.

Feeling at Peace with Me

Seasons change, yet they stay the same.
And my smile grows within.
For as I move forward, I take a minute to reflect,
even laugh, about where I have been…

My senses drift playfully through the colors in my life
…I see the greens as money and smell them as food…
…True blue as its gospel truth floating through the air
Icey crisp, mellow, moody, even soft without a care…

Flashes of red and white lightning stir my soul
as the sauciness of my surroundings flood my imagination.
Each color welcomes and rewards me
Each brings me a new sensation.

—-the beauty of black silk
—-the boldness of yellow gold
—-the sweet brown sound of chicken
—-a fragrant arrangement of orange bouquets
—-a relaxing red air of delight

When I allow me to be at peace with myself
I rejoice, knowing my gift of life is alright.

New Life

My Angel woke me up Again this morning.
And as we Spiritually Spoke, we Shared No words
Yet, as I Thought about my Need for Triumph and blessings…
The voice of Happiness is what I heard.

It was a New voice (True)
Full of Strength, yet Kind and Humble.
And it reminded me that the road to Success
Was created to make us Stumble.

Now, this voice advised me to replace my Stress with my Self
To build upon my Savior's gift of Treasure,
To recognize that not too deep within my Soul
Was a Knowing Heart, Supplied with grace beyond measure.

To Keep HATE out of my life
(Recognizing it as) Hurt Attached To Expectation…
Instead, to Try to be Honest, Amorous, Trusting, Energetic,
And reduce ongoing anger to momentary frustration.

For the blessing of Today makes yesterday more clear
The Holiness of this moment ignites my Soul so well.
I enjoy this Season of Thanksgiving
And Sing praise everyday for *Noel*.

I've got another chance to make a difference in my life
It could be my best, or even my last…
You see, my Angel woke me up again this morning
As it's done everyday, *Hallelujah*, in the past.

Two for Shore

Our tan is from within
For our giving
is a radiant source of our selves.

We share our time,
knowing its boundaries are incomplete,
And so much has changed
as we take our rightful seat.

The Word reclaims its place in my life.
As I inhale the breeze of God,
My spirit extends its reward

So I enjoy the background wind
Because I know a place where I can come
Where I'll float, yet I won't be bored.

Pressure: A Thing of the Past

Our most stressful moments are those in our minds
Where we worry about hardship or pain.
Yet, it is after we've recognized these moments as blessings
That we forget about winning or losing...
and enjoy being in the game.

We relax and recall the fragrance of that day,
Even that minute that we thought we wouldn't make it,
And smile at how we've blossomed, overcome and stayed alive.
We see ourselves as the diamonds we are...
who went through what we had to, to survive.

Our flashback sparkles with happy days and memories
Where 'pour' was what you did to season your food.
To days where people respected one another,
And even the oldest of kids was not rude.

What we depress is any vision that says we're lonely.
For our belief reminds us that we are only physically alone,
And it's our choice to look at our surroundings with sadness,
Or remember a certain crown of thorns, and a throne.

Each of our days become "Son" day
For to wake up is a blessing with no disguise.
To wake up is another chance to make a difference,
To eclipse new hurdles and become more wise.

We allow ourselves a bad moment.
But as a whole day, that moment cannot last.
Because we've proven we can take the pressure,
And that's why it's a thing of the past.

I Can't Save the World...
But I Can Save You.

Every time I talk to my mirror
My revelation is the same
I can't save the world
From all the injustice and the pain.

Yet, as I look around at the lives I touch
I'm reminded of something I fear
That my success might make me forget
About those who need me to care.

I could spend all my time with the media
And say that none of "them" are willing to work hard.
Or I can be thankful that I have the chance to make a difference
And recognize that chance as a grace from my God.

I can feed my spirit with my own personal thanks
Not "expecting" showers of praise from the people I serve
And I can relax knowing that I've done my best
Treating each person with the respect they deserve.

I can look back at the times I almost lost my temper
Now understanding that my disappointment was really concern
For who I thought was mature enough to take responsibility
Was actually only old enough to learn.

I can only help those who are willing to help themselves
By helping myself remain true
To the message I get from my mirror:
I can't save the world
But I can save you!

...human beings who helped me not lose sight of the grace that housed me on the side of the fence that labels me as administrators rather than recipients. And regardless of what your situation is in life, we're all going through *something*. The key...recognize that you're going through...

> *What I'm going through is not easy.*
> *It may get harder...it may get easier...*
> *what counts is what I decide to do with it.*
> *This is one more chance to take charge of my life.*
> *It may not be my last...it could be my best...*

Similar themes were used to create through the eyes of Senior Citizens. In October 1997, I began going around the city of Chicago speaking at Senior Citizen Centers of the Chicago Department on Aging. It was an intimidating undertaking...standing before senior citizens, suggesting how they might better enjoy their lives. My first visit to each of the centers started with my wondering whether or not they'd say "Come on, Sonny, we've heard all of that before..."

Each visit ended with thanks, nods of approval, even comments on how proud my mother must be of me. All of which encouraged me, and gave me the faith and courage to stand before "my seniors" and tell them that they needed to laugh, live, love and rest more. And as they agreed to do so, they reminded me to do the same.

These next 16 poems you'll read are those created through me by the words and thoughts of those who attended my monthly sessions. As so many people have heard seniors say "I've forgotten more than you'll ever remember...." we created a collection of poetry called *Remembering More Than You'll Ever Forget*. As you speak to a senior, you'll find this new statement to be true. And you'll need to remember to understand that they've seen and learned so much, that they have the "right" to forget some things without giving any credit to senility.

There were times where I wrote from the words they gave me…and times where we wrote together…using their names, favorite colors, numbers or expressions. Every time was a blessing. The words in either poem with capitalized first letters are those of the audience.

I remind you, as I reminded them, that if you have given birth to a child, volunteered your time or bought a raffle ticket to support a worthy cause…you have saved a life. Don't worry about counting each life; just know that you have saved many. Today you have the chance to save another…beginning with yours. Never forget that.

Love's Merry-Go-Round

You say tomato...I say tomotto
You say love...I say love
You say below...I say above.

What would life really be like if we were all on the same page?
If, as passengers, we saw no reason to turn
or change the scenary because "straight is good enough?"
What if we were all on the same page?

You say dias...I say dais
If, as observers, we appreciated only the opulence of the mountain,
with no regard for the trees, the sky and the clouds
that provide its majesty?
Or, as thinkers, we settled for the theory of least resistance,
agreeing that there are no options, no alternatives,
no need to consider one more route
(oh, I say route...You say root)
Would you only jump out of a plane with a designer parachute?

You see, our tastes are all the same—namely *different*.
Your opinion doesn't have to mirror mine.
so when dealing with a subject as complex as love
Agreeing that we may disagree is simply fine
(by the way, do you like red or white wine?)

See, love is in every relationship, each activity,
all we undertake and do
Love can easily be seen as fleeting...
Just as easily as it's felt as true.

It's a noun, it's a verb, it's an adverb.
The most misused used word in the English language
It's meaning evolves as daily as life unfolds
We believe in love when it's new
We question it when it's old.

Yet one thing we can agree on is that love belongs to our senses:
We see it…taste it…hear it…smell it…touch it…
We feel it, each of us in a different way.
And we can all agree that love goes up and love comes down.
The beauty is that it does it again,
with new passengers, like a merry go round.

You say nither…I say neether
What's important is that you say what you feel.
Love belongs to our senses
And to each of us it's as different as it is real.

God's Love

God's love never fails,
Though we sometimes expect it to...

We may sometimes feel incomplete.
And in that cavernous place of fantasy,
we lose sight of the true light that keeps us afloat.

A fantasy that should, instead,
invite us to a rainbow of joy
where the pot of gold at the end, is at the beginning.
Or have you forgotten that in the beginning,
there was the Word...

And just as the word was good,
so (too) must we believe in our wholeness:

Are you *W*illing to sacrifice...
happy to look success in the eye, and proclaim the victory?
Can you clear out yesterday and tomorrow...
to enjoy the *H*ere and now of this present?
Are you *O*n top of your game...
where you win because you compete only against yourself?
Do you *L*ove yourself?
And will the by-product of your love (Self Esteem)
bring you closer to the *E*verlasting passion and promise
of God's love...?

...for it never fails,
though we sometimes expect it to...

because we cannot understand his power.

Forgetting the Future...

Can you Forgive yourself for Forgetting what it was Like?
(For, how often have we actually made it to the Future?)
Sure, our words and Lives Forecast and Embrace
the Elusive tomorrow we longed for yesterday
and Live for today.
Yet we never quite get the handle on it, do we?

Oh, to go back and share the precious moments
that made us strongest...
To really pinpoint the day and time we Learned about Love.
Once through pain, twice through joy
Oh, what a Lesson.
When you thought to define yourself through the Eyes of others
And time and again your Expectations
threatened to stop someone else from being themselves
such that their reaction rejected your good intentions
And you retreated into Loving yourself,
Until you Found out just how important that was
to sharing in Love
And recognized the joy in Feeling
the Everlasting Love of Eternity.

Remember the First moment you understood "hot?"
Once the pain, twice the joy...
The second it took after the years, months, weeks,
days, hours and minutes
of protecting you from the Fullness of the Lesson
that there is a bitter/sweet reward in questioning authority,
As we were pampered into the reminder.

Can you Forgive yourself for Forgetting what it was Like?
How you Felt different depending upon who called you "boy"
or "girl"...
And turning the other cheek didn't seem Like much of a solution
By any means at all...
And even asking what you *haven't* done for this country,
seemed more appropriate?
Once through pain, twice through joy

Seasoned with JOY

The Songs we Sing Are Delightful to Our Spirit...
(it's Necessary that who we really Are, is Something we know)
they make us happy because we Deserve to be Aware of Our Options.
for we Are "Seasoned Citizens" Always on the go.

with a life to Share and Eyes to See
with the courage to Dare to be Obedient and free
to Enjoy the Oasis that builds our Solid ground
not Only Are we glad to be Alive...we're Oh, so happy to be Around.

because life is So Sweet, in fact it's Sweeter than honey
Some of us Share Our love, and Some Share Our Energy.
we Associate Ourselves with Excellence
and Our Ocean is filled with joy
we make Every Effort to grace the lives of each girl and Every boy.

the New challenge we face Everyday is getting up
you See, waking up is actually a breeze
we thank the Angel of Mercy (for, never the less)
we have the Opportunity to fall Down On Our knees.

the concept of OLD is Nice
we realize it means Onward Looms Dessert
it's Dear and Exciting to us
because it's where we Now happen to be
we can't Explain the Next hurdle
yet we know it's One that we'll See.

So, Seasoned with Joy is what we Are
Distinctive...Deserving...Delivered...Dynamic
you don't want us to Add Dangerous
So, Enjoy us as Seasoned Citizens
and remember (Above All) Adore us

Seniors Only

Oh, but won't that be the day?

Where everyone recognizes this gift
of patience...perseverance...prudence and wisdom...

Replacing the pain of unnecessary regret
with the memories of the goals that we've met.
Understanding the twinkle in each eye
even the blessing in being able to cry.

For what we seek is not mercy or sorrow,
but respect for our share in creating"tomorrow."
Realize that without us there'd be no such word
Understand that there's nothing we haven't heard.

We've made sacrifices, ends meet and through another day,
seen 'em come and go, near and far and always found a way.
Our peace of mind has been a piece of your's
Our joy a thing of beauty.
Each golden memory a reason to give thanks
Ever conscious of our duty.

So take this time to laugh with us
Sit a spell...share the majesty of this new day
Know that our happiness makes you smile
And our power cannot be taken away.

For we're here to pass the baton
We gladly watch you now run the race
We remind you to watch where you're going,
And to always be conscious of your pace.

Love Equals Peace

I can remember loving myself....
Actually, it was a long time ago,
And I didn't know it was love.
But I can remember the day...

    My steps had more confidence and vigor
And as I glided forward, certain people stepped out of my way.
My path was laid in gold and chock full of opportunity
And as I skipped ahead, several people helped me stay the path.

    My smile glistened in pearly white rays of hope
And as I enjoyed my ascension, many people returned a smile.
My thoughts danced in the comfortable blue background of honesty
And as I faced reality, a few people said "keep your head to the sky."

    Upon entering the Garden, my walk was upon red carpet
And as I confidently gathered myself to share my blessing
Someone told me I was black...poor...ignorant...

And I stopped loving me.

Yet, since I was no longer in love with me
I pushed myself harder to gain knowledge
And erase the ignorance.

Because I was no longer in love with me
I taught myself to manipulate wealth
And erase the poverty.

While I was no longer in love with me
I reminded myself to love you
And embrace the beauty and strength it takes to be me.

So, once again, my path beckons my walk
It will be a long walk,
    surrounded with happiness, content and wonderment
    And as I ease on down the road, everyone encourages me
    So I walk in peace....

Holy Rosa

Didn't we mention that the bus was only the beginning?
For this movement meant much more than a ride.
The strength in this woman was her obedience...
Yet her spirit was motivated by her pride.

Pride made a comment to Wisdom
Asked it *how necessary it was to lay low?*
Wisdom was no fool, it said *I'll go with you...*
Just promise me that you'll take it slow.

So they worked their way to the front of the bus
(these two...Pride & Wisdom)
They made no pause, as others watched and warned.
And as they sank into that seat that moment became everlasting
For never had authority been so scorned.

Fitting that her name was Rosa
For she rose above the pain that held so many back.
The pain that says slavery is mental
And it's favorite color never has been black.

Slavery's favorite color has always been ignorance...
Ignorance (somehow) continues to erase love.
As you take your ride in this lifetime (be smart)
Make sure the driver of your bus is up above

Renaissance Woman

She is wise beyond her years
A necessary part of my life
Optimistic…empathetic…to some, she's a mother
To others a sister, friend or wife.

Gazing at her across the table, I see my smile
And I am reminded of the part we play in one another's lives.
A role that goes beyond these walls
And rests in the spirit of moments shared, and words exchanged

…A noble spirit of ell-egance…
…A mar-ta of sun-ny delight…
…Like the lillies of the field, the jays in the ski…
…How-odd is-abell ringing at night…?

No way, Nance, can't fit you in this one
No matter how witty or efficient I may be.
But, like the others, you're an important piece of this puzzle
Each of you so bonded, yet so free.

How wonderful that your worlds have come together in this room
How perfect that your energies combine.
Remember to enjoy this spirit we nurture
And share your renaissance with all mankind.

Turning Points

If I wake up today, the exact same person I was yesterday
Perhaps I never went to sleep…

For, through the years, as my mind has hungered for knowledge
My curiosity has gotten the best of me,
Even when I gave it no target…
And my ability to understand yesterday
Fuels the happiness I continuously plan to enjoy.

A happiness and joy I accept into my life
In as many ways as possible,
Recognizing its short and long term intentions in retrospect.

I hold onto each moment
Outwardly bold, courageous, and determined…
(While inside afraid, bewildered, and cautious)
And my belief system asks that I acknowledge my fortune
And reward myself for mastering change as I have.

Though I can't remember the first step or fall I've taken,
I recall the last.
Unable to quote each word I've spoken or heard,
I share my wisdom…recount all I've learned.
I've refused to give in…turned down offers…missed an opportunity
Forgotten & Forgiven…Loved & Lost…Won & Wondered
And my belief system asks that I acknowledge my spirituality
And reward myself for mastering change as I have.

Since I reached my first goal this morning (waking up)
I've lived each minute and second unlike the last
And as I focus on what I'm good at and what I like about myself
I live for the present, not the past.

For I could have surrendered a long time ago
Instead I chose to stay,
To brace myself for the next turning point
And call it "yesterday."

Women

...Can't live without them (period)
And I wouldn't want to have to be the one to prove it...

Thus, as I sat beside the fireplace last night,
my thoughts drifted to you.
Not the words we exchanged during our last time together,
but to *you*.

And as I listened to the crackle of the wood
I was reminded of the crispness and effervescence of your smile...
A glow of encouragement, inspiring me to breathe
and enjoy this walk of faith.

Staring into the dancing flames
I saw the many faces of your beauty, and sensed your moods...
As you stare into the mirror we now share.

Funny, how it seems I have a message...
When I am merely the messenger.
Clever, how I mouth your words...
With no sight of your hand running up my back.
Lasting, your affect on the lives you touch...
Neither beginning nor ending with mine.

Oh, I could go on...
But, I can't *live* without you (period)

Flame of Life

She stood out from the rest…because she was mine…

Oh, how I enjoyed her touch and soothing words
The way she handled me like no one else could or dared.
What was mine has been her's since the day I recognized her
And our love has never ceased, only subsided.

We've enjoyed the ups and downs, ins and outs, good and bad times.
So often she's gone that extra mile for me
with no expectation or doubt
In fact, when you really get down to it
She's the one who knows what I'm all about.

Though it hasn't been every waking moment of our lives
We've made up for the time we were apart.
And I know that I'll always love her
Not with words…but deep in my heart.

She is Wonderful, wise and her thoughts are always with me
She is Omni-present and reminds me she'll be there for me
She is Mary, Mary Ann, Merry, My one and only
She is Energetic, my everlasting love
She is Necessary, nice, nosey (it's true)

She's a part of the flame in my life
Who is She to you?

Thirst for Life

Inner thoughts are refreshing
Because they touch on realism and hope.
They inspire the impossible…intriguing and realistic…
And take us to new adventures.

Helping us see ourselves as powerful role models
Whose anticipation can't be denied
Because I've been there, done that, and succeeded
While others have not even tried.

Wellness is at the top of our minds
For we aspire to be healthy, rewarding and rich…
But what does "rich" mean?

It's the resolution to do better
the rejoicing of the outcome
the radiance that follows…

As we dream
the possible becomes real
As we live
we fulfill those dreams
For everything is really possible
When we focus on our 'being!'

My thirst is for life
Ah! Because I am an angel
And my touch is nurturing,
And sometimes even good advice.
Because I know I'm not infallible
But I know that I'm very nice!

Respect

We receive it when we aim to give it
If our attitude is intact.
Respect is a blessing that is learned
And it helps us all interact.

It's a universal feeling that we all need
Necessary…Natural…Nice
And it's favor, not luck
Respect requires patience when we remember whose we are
to refrain from running "a-muck."

It should be everyone's intention
It's in everybody's best interest
And it's our highest human choice
It's a way of encouraging our spirituality
And reminding us to rejoice.

For to live without respect would be
Disastrous…Devastating…Demoralizing
Because we need it (that's all!)
And everyone deserves it again and again.

Respect is a key to good living
And to our lives
Amen…Amen…Amen

Reign of Excellence

Oh, it's coming down, no need to worry or fret
What you really need to know, is how to relax and not get wet...

The wetness is perspiration
Brought about by worry...agonizing...and pain...
While the fragrant breeze of independence
Is a refreshing taste of all we gain.

Our gain finds us as newborn prophets
Though human, intelligent beyond even our years.
We've listened and learned for a life time
And through grace we've hurdled much fear.

Our actions have outweighed our losses
As achievement has been our proving ground.
We've been there, done, got the tee shirt and washed it
And it's obvious to see we're still around.

We're around because our blessings have been answered
We're moving forward, invigorated and radiant with grace
We're independent, intelligent, even amorous
Ever worthy of His excellence in our space.

For God has shown us several sides of the coin,
Reminded us of what we should spend and how:
Time with one another...each loved one...
Happilly...and now.

So, come, let's walk in the reign
It's a "bow" that will never leave us standing alone.
It's the reign-bow of excellence,
And it's glow will always take you home.

Giving

There's only one True originating point
That place is called your Heart
There dwells a Kindred Spirit
And a child who won't Age,
but ever grows Smart.

That child's Neighbors are Angels,
full of Hope and opportunity…
Their golden roads lead Happilly to the King.
For as we give, we catch up to what we've received
We share our life, our love, our laughter
and Trust in who we believe.

We Keep our Smile Aglow with Sincerity
Our Touch, ever gentle and reassuring.
In fact we become so Humble and Silent
That Some might consider us boring.

Yet it is because we are calm that we prosper.
What we give most Absolutely is our Thanks
Our wisdom has helped us pass the Test of Time
Time more precious than the money in the bank.

There's only one True originating point
It's the nucleus of our dreams,
Saving us to See Another day.
Open your Hands in praise to Heaven's glory
For, what you give can never be taken Away.

As you can see, throughout this book, a major part of what I do is manipulating words. Though our society often asks for a negative price tag on *manipulate*, part of its definition is *to manage or use skillfully*. We have to be extremely conscious of using words to our best advantage, because words are powerful. In fact words are so powerful that they sometimes dictate how we feel, and determine how others see us.

Of course, it's more crucial for you to have a clear recognition of who you are and how important you are to the lives of those you touch. And realize that you touch more lives than you can count. Those that you can count, need you to stay positive and add your piece to the puzzle that makes their lives complete (as we need them to complete ours).

Not every rainbow is found in the sky.
When we ground ourselves properly in the Lord,
blessings become our cushion
rather than our shield.

Yet, too often we take ourselves for granted. We don't acknowledge this gift of life that gives us the power to comfort and control. We surrender ourselves to the *lesson* we learned that says we have to be humble. A true enough lesson…when we recognize that our humility does not require bowing to mankind, or quieting ourselves in public. Being humble means giving thanks to God…and acknowledging our inability to prosper without faith. When people call you self-centered or conceited, let them know they've misread the fact that you're self-confident and convinced!

In the fall of 1999, I had the opportunity to become Artist-In-Residence at Purdue University's Black Cultural Center…working with one of their four ensembles: The Haraka Writers.

As you get in touch with your personal power, you develop a picture of yourself that becomes more comfortable with outwardly expressing that joy. Inside, we are absolutely crazy about ourselves. That's why we brush our teeth, wash and dress—things that we think we do by habit. The fact of the matter is that we love ourselves far more than words can express. Though these "habits" seem small, they are bonafide examples of our subconscious pride in presenting and projecting the image of who we are.

In fact, take a moment to look in the mirror and give you a wink (everyday). It's the greatest pick-me-up you can find. And don't wait until you're having a bad *time* (remember, there are no bad *days*) to give this a try. Do it now, while you think I've got to be out of my mind to suggest it. You'll laugh at the thought of your doing it. Yet, the key becomes for you to get comfortable with enjoying your *self*, and inspiring you to keep moving forward. As you meet people by design, not coincidence, do your part to share your message and receive theirs.

Young Prophets

Vibes.
Vibes that float on fresh gusts of air
and land on that part of your body
that gives the greatest sense of satisfaction:
your mind.

Oh, I know you're still fighting the stereotype
that says they're kids,
Or that what they have to share is wisdom
(without the "wizzzz")

Stereotypes
that say they all come from the same place
and are headed in the same direction:
Somewhere & Nowhere…
Vibes.

Vibes that float on warm gusts of air
and land on that sensual part of your body
that gives the greatest sense of extreme satisfaction:
your mind.

And it's okay.
I know you skipped that phase in your life
that flooded in subconscious cries
for guidance (not directions)…
and you lost track, or got cheated out of
being responsible for your present
and impacting your future…
by someone caught up in their past. [chuckle]
Vibes.

Vibes that float on cool gusts of air
and land on that sensitive part of your body
that gives the greatest sense of perceived satisfaction
and reminds you that I must share all I have: Me!

And through that sharing I land where I can do you the most good:
your mind.

Giving a Stand

See, you can't always take one.
Yet, your opinion must be expressed
So, what becomes key is the fullness of your source...
For what will happen when your voice is heard?
Will many follow you and thrive?
Or find themselves begging to stay alive?

Have you done a power check lately,
And found a hush come over the room when you spoke?
Would you switch places with me right now
Or can you feel me enough to give me a smile?
And don't just smile…breathe.
Breathe and let that breath settle you down to ask another question:
Will the people who love you most desert you
When you decide to give a stand?
See, you can't always take one.

When you give a stand
Will you tap into a place within yourself that you hadn't felt?
A place flushed with light
exposing emotions of professed blackness?
Oh, come on…you know the blackness I'm talking about
Not the Stevie Wonder Livin' Just Enough For the City
New York Just Like I Pictured It Get In the Cell…Blackness…
That has led us from one generation to the next,
With only the faces changed to protect the names of the innocent.
You see I'm dealing with and talking about
The blackness of ignorance.

Ignorance that gets you mad enough to call someone a blind M/F
(you know, not knowing whether they're Male or Female)
Because what has happened in their lives
Is that they've chosen to block out, to be blind to
what has happened in their lives.
So they find the need to treat people as the demons that haunt them
And conjure up memories that "justify" their lust for revenge.
You see their ignorance is so strong
That they have no clue what it might be like
To give a stand.
Because you can't always take one.

But if people like you,
Who've decided to give the first step
and listen to what we have to say,
Choose to give the next step and do what you have to do,
What we've chosen to give you tonight
will not fall upon deaf hearts.
Hearts and spirits unafraid of the challenge
of personal belief and commitment.
You see, when you decide to give a stand
what becomes key is the fullness of your source…
Because you might find
that your life becomes immersed in questions.

When you give a stand
Will you be able to answer them?

Through a speaking engagement in 1997, I became introduced to a disease called Reflex Sympathy Dystrophy (RSD). I was told by a woman who had RSD that it was like a cross between cancer and muscular dystrophy. And that the pain was sometimes so intense, that clapping caused discomfort. I would later speak to an RSD support group after creating the following poem in their honor.

Proclaim the Victory

I see you as you are, because I know where I have been
I reach out to remind you that in the spirit, is where joy must begin.

Yes, work has gotten on my nerves
I've gotten sick of certain twists of fate
I've been bored, insensitive, and disbelieving...
but wait!

I've been excitable, empathetic,
(oh) even naive
Enjoyed watching you get ahead,
and pleased with all you've achieved.
In fact, we've lived through one another, taken turns setting the pace.
Still, you have always gotten us farther,
even through this trauma I face.

For suddenly I realize that my reminders are to myself
How gifted I am just to be
And whether my prayers go up or come down
I remind myself that it is You with me.

Recognizing that fact, I find comfort, even joy in my pain
(Of course "*find joy*" and "*enjoy*" are in no way the same)

Yet, I know you keep it to a minimum.

And though there are times where it drives me insane
my tears saturate the wisdom of loved ones,
and quench the memories of things I've already done:
serious accomplishments, wild & crazy love affairs, sports, cooking,
dancing, trick or treating, winning, losing, and good old childish fun.

So I remind myself that I am a child of God
I remember that only He can take care of me.
Yes, I see You as You are, because You've sent me where I've been
I reach out to acknowledge that in Your spirit,
is where all joy must begin.

Joy must begin in your spirit, as well. What *types* of things have happened in your life that you have mistaken for sadness...before allowing them to blossom into the joy of your metamorphosis? In fact, so often it is through misfortune that we receive the true message of our being. Yet, we all start out needing someone else to justify our message, as you will see in the upcoming poem. As you read it, recognize that you are beautiful. And as we mature we come to realize that...

Beauty Is in the "I"

I am beautiful...
    Largely because your spirit of sharing
    and expression of concern for my well-being
    has given my cheeks a flush of childish joy,

I am beautiful...
    And through that sensation
    the stimulation of my love of self is heightened,

I am beautiful...
    For as I come to understand my affect on your life
    I grow beyond unseen boundaries
    to realize, yes even recognize,
    the cerebral euphoria of our exchange.

I am beautiful...
    And as I enjoy my beauty,
    my longing for your acceptance begins to cease...
    in its place, there is joy.

    I am beautiful.

Every Life, a Young Life

Does Mom lose her title as the years go by…
Can Dad no longer be someone's brother?
When God summons us to His home
It's not because we're old, young or "other."

For each of us starts the day anew
With memories of lessons, not regrets.
Today is another chance for me to be a part of your life
To let my memory help you pass another test.

It's called the test of time,
And we've all passed it.
Eventually, it passes us all
Though I'll not be there now when you call me, smile
For you were always there when I called.

Every life is a young life
For we each wake to start a new day.
So lets rejoice and make the most of the time we share,
For our memories will never go away

I Am Here Today

I am here today.
Give me hugs
Hold me in your arms
Kiss me on my head
Save me from harm.

I am here today.
Tell me you love me
Show me that you do
One day I'll make history
And I'll owe it all to you.

I am here today.
Treat me as you want to be treated
Call me by my name
Help me respect you
This is my life,
Not a game.

I am here today.

As I always remind people, we share only mental moments. How often have you been somewhere, only to later comment that you "...were there physically, but [your] mind was somewhere else..." That's why it's so important to let positive thoughts govern your imagination. One day, both you and another person will have a final thought of one another. What would you like those thoughts to be?

I'm Thinking about You Today.

I'm on a flight to New York...

The wind is beating against the plane,
squeezing that capsule first,
then passing its pressure on to my shoulders.

I'm thinking about your cry and my laugh.

No, I don't have a death wish,
but I love you now.

I don't mind sharing my life with you
because [believe me]
if I could—I'd share my death.

Wow, wouldn't that be cool?
We'd both be 1/2 alive,
and have a more full appreciation
for what it means to be whole (wouldn't we?)...

...Everything now is okay.

Friendship Questioned & Answered

Can I call you "friend"
If my understanding cannot fathom
the gamut of my responsibility?

And will you call me "friend"
When my love for you becomes so shallow and self-serving
That our conversation
Becomes no more than a volleyed measuring of phraseology?

When I don't know your mood,
My shoulder and ear has a "Reserved for You" sign
To welcome your tears, fears and laughter.

When I know your mood,
I dare not share any less.

Friendship Disguised as Love

Let me remind you
That you are privy to my true self,
When others see me smile, you know how I pain inside
For you, I forgive my ceasing
The masquerade associated with pride.

To you I'll admit loss
While many hear only of my gain,
So obviously with you this close to me
I can be predictable and rhyme with the word "pain."

Let remind you
That you are privy to my true moods,
And you have often been the true source of my joy.
Thus, while others salute and praise me
or call me "Mr. Man"
You poke me and just say "You Go Boy."

Let me remind you
That you are privy to my soul,
And my spirit often functions in your favor
You are a wonderful person brought into my life
Our love disguised as friendship is one I'll always savor.

State of Mind

My best days don't always make me smile
Instead I enjoy a comfort deep inside.
My mind drifts to that customer who thanked me
Who acknowledged my professionalism and pride.

Overshadowed is the Raging Redhead,
Who so hotly contested my quote
I can laugh at the Babbling Brunette
And the pain that I heard in that throat

See, I can imagine them falling off of the wrong side of the bed
And I resist the temptation to sell them insurance
For that bump on their shoulders—their head.

For I know what it's like to have a bad day
And I thank God that I've had a few
I've been blessed with the patience of Job
And my policy on joy is renewed.

My spirit reminds me to take stock in what I'm doing
To believe in myself as no one else would
I wink in the mirror, sit back and trust myself
Because I know that I am that good.

So often we want to justify trials and tribulations in our lives as acts of the devil. The twists, turns and drops in my life have all come compliments of God's love for me...and mine for God. There is no other power at work in my life. The deeper I look within, the more joy I find in sharing my gift with you. May these closing poems remind you to stay the path of faith that has delivered you today...the final one having been performed as a Thanksgiving invocation before feeding the homeless in 1997.

Know that each of us is in place right now to save a life. Know that there is no life more important to save than your own, because yours is an intrinsic message that simply must be shared.

What Happens When We Leave God Out of Love?

What happens when we leave God out of love?
What happens to those around us…
What can we really do…
What will we really have to share…
What happens to me and you?

What happens when we leave God out of love?
How can we share or be happy…
How does that make us feel…
How can our relationships remain true…
How will we know love is real?

What happens when we leave God out of love?
Where do we find ourselves…
Where is our light…
Where is that feeling of satisfaction…
Where is that knowledge that says this is right?

What happens when we leave God out of love?
Why does our heart become covered with hate…
Why don't we care…
Why are we so cold…
Why do we let love's freshness become stale,
and then let it become old?

What happens when we leave God out of love?
Who are we really cheating…
Who has the most at stake…
Who
Whose heart really breaks?

When we leave God out of love
there are no answers…only questions.
Questions that lead to doubt
So before you call it "love"
make sure you know what He's all about

Power Unveiled

When we realize how truly powerful we are
We must now overcome fear...

When I wanted, I saw what to strive for.
As my need grew, I knew just what to do.
And now that I'm there, I must choose what I can share.

For the air up here is new,
And its exhilaration is not so unfamiliar to my ego .
Nor uncomfortable to my touch .
unpalatable to my taste .
illogical or unrecognizable.

Yet my neighbors are doubt, disbelief and caution.
And as I consider their comfort
They exhibit more unrest,
And I become prone to shut them out.

Instead, I invite them up.

How Far Is the Middle?

How far is the middle…
    Have you run this race before…
        Do you know how to be a winner…
            Or do you just know how to score?

Our lives move forward at a pace set by words
Where all things we're about to…
        getting ready to…
        thinking about doing, can get the last laugh
When we put our breathing on hold to explain/justify indecision.

How far is the middle…
    Have you run this race before…
        Do you know how to be a winner?
            You can fly or you can soar.

See, when our lives are so cut and dry…
            black and white…
            hot or cold…
We find ourselves surrounded by options that possess a new clarity
Though we can't recognize or acknowledge it
A clarity that thirsts
for connection, understanding, empathy, flexibility, joy, reward, truth, love…
"…you know what I'm saying…"

How far is the middle…
    Have you asked Him to keep your score?
        For you know how to be a winner…
            You can fly or you can soar.

Our starting and ending points mean little.
What we've done to get here is what counts.
Let us be thankful for the experience,
Even the blessing to look back and see
The lessons of life learned our way,
That shape us and help us to be.

How close are you to God…
    Have you asked Him to keep your score?
        For you know how to be a winner…
            You can fly or you can soar.

The Wish

Each outstretched hand is cloaked in a hidden bond
It's grip as satisfying as a caress.
When we touch, sharing becomes the magic
For we help one another do more with less.

You see, sometimes "wish"
is the sound of someone passing us by
or an expression used to remind us to give up.
And then there are times where the "W" stands for We
and someone is there to help us fill our cup.

Oh sure, the "I" could be for Ignore
the "SH" for Sugar, Honey [of Iced Tea].
But the blessing of a wish is to look around at God
And enjoy all that He has let you see.

Each outstretched hand is cloaked in a hidden bond
It's caress as satisfying as a grip.
By sharing the magic in your touch
You've given my cup one more sip.

Cloudy Daze

Today I watched the majesty of the clouds move
as they rested in pantomime against the blue ceiling

At least I think it was blue.

See, blue is what I saw
And in life sometimes all we see are colors
instead of how well they work together.

How brown will stand still for green to grow.
Green invites yellow, even burnt orange or red
Then red returns the favor
by pulling out all the stops to go through yellow
and become one with green.

But…I know what you're thinking:
What about gray…?
Because sometimes it's the master of our day.
Well, not really…
We just let it feel that way.

Where we lose focus
and allow the condescending haze of doubt
to conjure up colorless shades of ignorance
that flash around us and rape our imagination of its luster.
Without a doubt, gray does this by choice
yet it also invites us to recognize it
as the midpoint between two extremes:
black and white…

Reminds us that there can be the perfect blend of sharing
if we're willing to keep the scale from losing its balance.

Today I watched the majesty of the clouds move
as they rested in pantomime against the blue ceiling
And I was reminded
that in life sometimes all we see are colors
instead of how well they work together.

Levels of Presidency

Some of us are in charge of companies…
others, just our families and ourselves.
Thus, we're all at some level of presidency
So the real question is *"What's on your shelves?"*

Are your shelves filled with old ideas
With volumes and volumes about how you won't change?
Or is there just a little less dust on each chapter of your life
To confirm that you have rearranged?
Rearranged priorities…shifted opinions…
even grown from constructive feedback.
And do your shelves say you've benefited or lost
because your heritage revealed that you're Black?

Are your shelves—tall?
I don't want to say "high" because I'm not talking about
what you may like to get
to allow your mind to drift away from my truth.
Because my truth attacks you in a silent spot that has a sign saying
"Please See The Head Librarian"
In other words, a spot that you don't truly want to share
Because you don't truly want to be set free…are your shelves—tall?
With volumes and volumes of tales about what you
could've done…might've been…or should've had
if only your stories didn't let your scapegoat be the hero?
And have they gotten too tall for you to recognize yourself as
tapped on the shoulder by grace
that saved you from sitting on the *"Have Not"* side of the fence?
Or are your shelves tall
Because each of us here respects your *Top Shelf* mentality?
We support your worthiness, value and reputation
of being head & shoulders above the rest.

So we read on about you, smile and occasionally look back
Never once deciding that you benefited or lost
simply because you're Black.

Are your shelves as filled on the left as they are on the right?
Are your morals and values in visible sight?
Are the things we should really know about you neatly filed away…
Or do we get to read about your viewpoints,
and quote what you have to say?
Can we enjoy you as a novel, laugh at your comic books
Thumb through the photo albums, enjoy the memories
and the evolution of your *look*?
Will we give you the credit you deserve without attack
And recognize there's no benefit or loss, you're just good
In your case, you happen to be Black.
And some of us are in charge of companies…
others, just our families and ourselves.
You see, we're all at some level of presidency
So the real question is *"What's on your shelves?"*

Silent Fanfare

How can I help you live today?
Shall I jump up and scream
"Follow the plan!"...
And, if I did, could you keep the pace
And understand that it's God's will,
Not that of man?

Need I take your hand
and press it against every beating heart
to remind you of the many lives you touch?
Or can I simply ask for one more breath
To insist that you lay down your crutch?

For this walk among mortals
is an exercise in trust...
Our goal is not getting from Point A to Z.
Instead, our goal is making the point
of getting all we need from G-O-D.

Through each set of eyes and hearts
Today I will get my well deserved share
While my smile and pose of comfort
Cheers for you through your blessing and prayer.

Let your tears represent the joy in this victory
As your memory flashes back to all we've won
Don't spend my visible moments in sadness
Instead, have one more tribute to our fun.

I Miss Me

I thought about switching lives with you.
But I miss me already.

See, I don't know if you enjoy waking up every morning
And that happens to be one of my favorite moments
Because it starts me off having reached my primary goal of the day
For my goal everyday is to wake up tomorrow…

And I don't know if you really appreciate
how your fingers and toes move.
While I know I really get a kick out of feeling
solid, soft or sandy soil supporting my successful stride.
I happen to enjoy touching, squeezing, holding
and pointing myself in the right direction
That direction is up, (by the way) are you headed that way?
I know I am,
And I'd sure like to be in my shoes when I get there…
Because I pretty much know how I'd deal with the crowds.

Got my acceptance speech ready, and been practicing my smile
Come to think of it,
I've been working on it since I was a child.
My favorite outfit will be pressed brand new
Family, friends, teachers, heroes, TV shows,
clients, habits and hobbies
They'll all be there too.
Can't say I'd know how to handle them all,
if I woke up and found out I was you.

My mentors would take credit, while giving me praise
They'd help me relive memories and cherish new days
Oh, how I would laugh at the tough times
and the material things that were lost
And rejoice in the character they helped build
See, my life and spirit are beyond monetary cost.

Every enemy would stand in their place
and receive equal time to express the beauty they inspired
through their negativity.
Let's face it,
so many of the lessons we actually learn come from disharmony.
A selfish person made me want to share…
A jealous person helped me recognize insecurity…
A lie reminded me to tell the truth…
I remember joy & pain…I like sunshine & rain…
And it was a man who taught me how to be a man.

I've been vigilant, patient, spontaneous, loving, mean, mischievous.
Ignorant, irresponsible, (irresistible), innocent, intelligent,
intuitive, intimate, interesting, introspective/indecisive, insightful/
insatiable, insensitive/incredible, indispensable, independent,
incoherent/incognito, indescribable, inexperienced, infallible,
indestructible, inspirational, inquisitive, instinctive, instrumental,
IN…and OUT…
Outstanding/outrageous, outside/outsmarted, outspoken/outdone,
outlandish/outclassed, outwitted/outcast, outnumbered, outraged,
outright, outreached, outranked, outvoted, outgoing, out of sight,
out of this world…
oh, yes, even out of breath…(and almost) out of my mind.

Because, I thought about switching lives with you.
But I miss me already.

See, I don't know if you enjoy waking up every morning,
And that happens to be one of my favorite moments.

Thanks-Living

So often our thanks drift toward dreams
and hopes and wishes and wants.
And so often we look past the beauty and gift of NOW.

For, as we point to our village for future leaders,
We sometimes look beyond the reality
of the fact that cultivation begins in the present…

Blindly we chastise every move we make,
question our reason for being,
doubt our faith in God.

We show ourselves as role models of failure,
Rather than the masters of persistence and perseverance we are,
Where we should be encouraging our children
to step up to success.

Understand that God gives us children
to stretch our learning capability…
Pray that they go beyond you,
Rather than hope they get as far…
Have you not taken your true Father's hand?

And as you listen to what you say,
Hear how you say it.

Is yours the voice of defeat…shame…forgetfulness?
Oh, have you forgotten the blessing of each day
On this side of the ground?

Can you see your hand?
Thank You, Father

Can you touch your ear?
Thank You, Father
Can you hear your voice?
Thank You, Father
Can you say "Hurry up, Sporty, this food smells good?
Thank You, Father
Can you breathe in the blessing of this meal?
Thank You, Father.

For just as there is a time
where we are all one step away from homelessness

There is also a time
where we must all believe that we are one step away
from *living* true thanks.

And all the people said: *AMEN*

*Today I took a moment to enjoy my life
I looked around,
counted each blessing I could find.
Then I looked for blessings I couldn't see.*

Your name came to mind.